Pirate Attack!

Withdrawn

By Deborah Lock

US Senior Editor Shannon Beatty
Senior Editor Caryn Jenner
Editor Nandini Gupta
Art Editors Emma Hobson, Shruti Soharia Singh
Jacket Editor Francesca Young
Jacket Designers Amy Keast
DTP Designer Anita Yadav
Picture Researcher Aditya Katyal
Producer, Pre-Production Nadine King
Producer Niamh Tierney
Managing Editor Laura Gilbert
Deputy Managing Editor Vineetha Mokkil
Managing Art Editors Diane Peyton Jones, Neha Ahuja Chowdhry
Art Director Martin Wilson
Publisher Sarah Larter
Publishing Director Sophie Mitchell

Reading consultant Linda Gambrell, Ph.D.

First American Edition, 2017
Published in the United States by DK Publishing
345 Hudson Street, New York, New York 10014

Copyright © 2017 Dorling Kindersley Limited
DK, a Penguin Random House Company
17 18 19 10 9 8 7 6 5 4 3 2 1
001—306513—Jun/17

Published in Great Britain by Dorling Kindersley Limited.

A CIP catalog record for this book is available from the Library of Congress.

ISBN: 978-1-4654-6473-6 (Paperback)
ISBN: 978-1-4654-6474-3 (Hardcover)

DK books are available at special discounts when purchased in bulk for sales promotions, premiums, fund-raising, or educational use. For details, contact:
DK Publishing Special Markets
345 Hudson Street, New York, New York 10014
SpecialSales@dk.com

Printed and bound in China.

The publisher would like to thank the following for their kind permission to reproduce their photographs:
(Key: a-above; b-below/bottom; c-center; f-far; l-left; r-right; t-top)

All other images © Dorling Kindersley
For further information see: www.dkimages.com

A WORLD OF IDEAS:
SEE ALL THERE IS TO KNOW

www.dk.com

Contents

Words in **bold** appear in the glossary.

Get Ready to Sail

A long time ago, pirates sailed the seas. They took **treasure** from other ships. Pirates loved gold and other treasure.

"Ahoy, matey!" That's how pirates said hello in olden times.

Ahoy! I'll tell you all about pirates.

Pirate
Ship

mast

sail

rudder

hull

These are the
main parts of a ship.

rigging

main deck

Chapter 1

Setting Sail

A pirate ship needed a captain and **crew**. The captain was in charge. The crew had different jobs. Sometimes, children worked in pirate crews. They even got a small share of the treasure.

One of the most famous pirates was Blackbeard. People were scared to fight with Blackbeard. That made it easier for him to steal their treasure.

Blackbeard had many pirate ships. His biggest ship was called *Queen Anne's Revenge*.

Wanted Dead or Alive!

Blackbeard

Real name: **Edward Teach**

(Beware! He is very dangerous.)

"Hoist the sails" means to put them up so the wind can blow the ship along.

When it was time to set sail, the pirate captain gave the orders.

"Lift the anchor!"

"Hoist the sails!"

The crew pulled up the **anchor** and raised the sails. Then the ship sailed out to sea!

Pirate Rules

Here are some rules that pirate crews had to follow.

 Obey the captain.

 No fighting on board the ship.

 Keep **weapons** clean and ready for battle.

 Lights out at 8 o'clock at night.

PIRATES WHO BROKE THE RULES WERE PUNISHED!

These were some punishments.

 Painful lashes with a whip.

Help!

Ouch!

 Being left alone on an island.

Bang!

 Being shot with a pistol.

Chapter 2
Life on Board

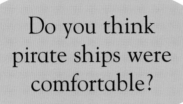

Do you think
pirate ships were
comfortable?

Life could be hard on board
a pirate ship. Pirates were at sea
for a long time. They often slept in
hammocks below **deck**. There were
plenty of rats below deck, too.

Pirates couldn't
be picky about
their food!

Pirates had to eat whatever the ship's cook prepared. Fresh food started to rot after a while. Then the pirates ate food that had been dried or covered with salt. This made the food last longer.

Pirate Food

Pirates often spent months at sea, so they needed food that would last.

salt

sacks of grain

salted meat

Limes and other citrus
fruits kept pirates healthy,
but soon rotted.

citrus fruit

barrels
of food

dried fruit

There was a lot of work to do on a pirate ship. The crew made sure the ship was in good condition so it didn't sink. They scrubbed the decks and kept the ship clean.

Pirates also had fun. They
played musical instruments and
sang songs called **sea shanties**.
They often sang sea shanties while
they worked.

Pirate Sea Shanty

Pretend you're on a pirate ship and sing this sea shanty!

A pirate's life is the life for me.
Yo ho ho and a bottle of rum!
On a ship so fine we'll sail out to sea.
Yo ho ho and a bottle of rum!

Here with my hearties, we'll travel the waves,
And those who cross us end up in their graves.

We fight to the last.
We are brave and so bold,
And share out the treasure
of glittering gold.

So sing loud the tune and
bang on the drum.
Yo ho ho and a bottle of rum!

In this sea shanty,
which words rhyme
with rum and gold?

What was the treasure?

What is a heartie?

25

Chapter 3

Battle at Sea

Sometimes, a pirate climbed up to the top of the ship to look out to sea. He could see a long way from up there! If a pirate spotted another ship, he called out, "Sail ho!"

That was the signal. The pirate captain would order his crew to get their weapons ready.

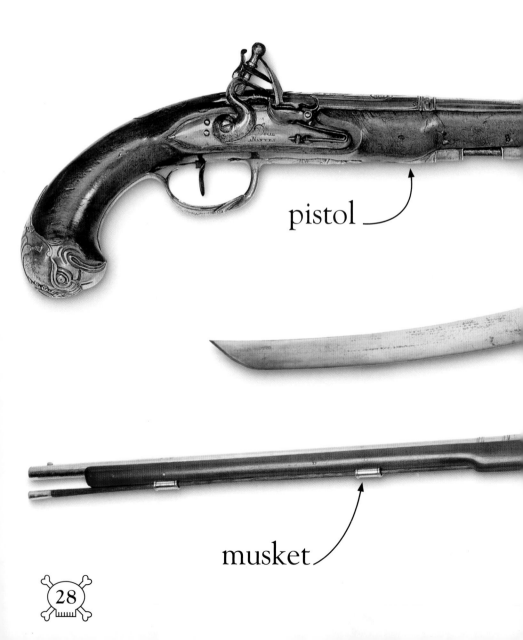

pistol

musket

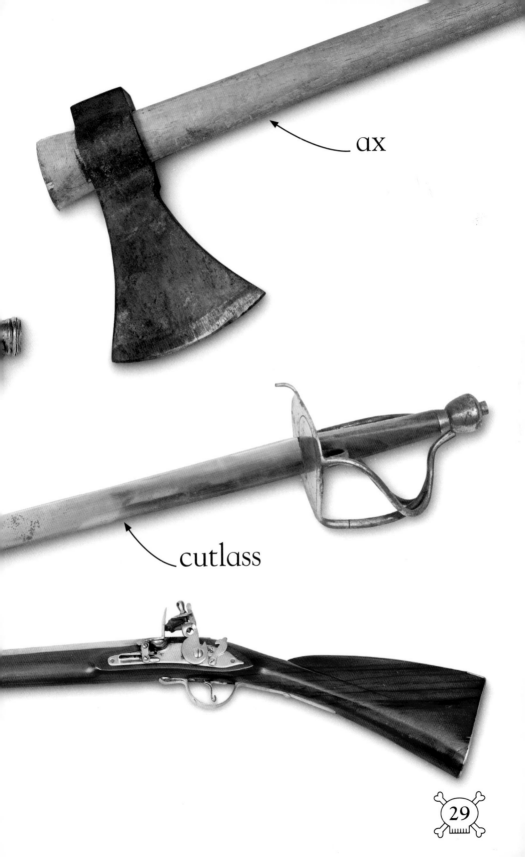

ax

cutlass

Pirate ships flew a black flag
called a Jolly Roger. The Jolly
Roger warned other ships that
pirates were coming!

The pirates hoped that the crew of the other ship might give up. That way the pirates could take their treasure without a fight.

If the other crew didn't give up, then the pirates attacked. First they fired the cannon.

Bang!

Pirates went to sea to rob other ships. They weren't afraid of fighting to get what they wanted—treasure!

Treasure

Most ships carried **cargo** such as sugar and spices. Pirates could sell these things for money. Of course, the best kind of treasure was gold!

sugarcane

coins

spices

Chapter 4

Sailing Away

After a battle, the pirates sailed away to find more treasure. Sometimes, the seas were stormy. Choppy waves tossed their ships this way and that. The pirates had to steer the ship carefully so it didn't sink!

Sometimes, the pirates saw land in the middle of the sea. Then they could stop sailing for a while. They could repair the ship. They might find food and supplies, too.

Land ahoy!

Some pirates sailed to deserted islands. No one lived on these islands. Many people think that pirates buried their treasure on deserted islands.

The idea of buried treasure probably came from books such as **Treasure Island**, by Robert Louis Stevenson. However, most pirates didn't really bury their treasure. They spent it or traded it for other things. Pirates were too greedy!

Pirate Lingo

Pirates had their own way of speaking. Here are some pirate words and expressions.

Yo ho ho!
(Said when happy)

Ahoy, mateys!
(Hello, friends!)

Ahoy! Did you know that most real pirates did not have pet parrots?

Seadog
(An old pirate)

Heave ho!
(Push)

Pieces of eight
(Coins)

Shiver me timbers!
(Said when shocked)

Booty!
(Treasure)

Pirate Quiz

1. How did pirates say "hello" in olden times?

2. What was Blackbeard's real name?

3. What does "hoist the sails" mean?

4. What did pirates sleep in?

5. What was the Jolly Roger?

 Answers on page 48.

Glossary

anchor something heavy used to stop the ship from moving

cargo things taken from one place to another on a ship

crew people working on a ship

deck floor of a ship

sea shanties songs sung by sailors

treasure things that are worth a lot of money

Treasure Island famous book about pirates written in 1883

weapons tools for fighting

Guide for Parents

This book is part of an exciting four-level reading series for children, developing the habit of reading widely for both pleasure and information. These chapter books have a compelling main narrative to suit your child's reading ability. Each book is designed to develop your child's reading skills, fluency, grammar awareness, and comprehension in order to build confidence and engagement when reading.

Ready for a *Level 2* book

YOUR CHILD SHOULD

- be familiar with using beginning letter sounds and context clues to figure out unfamiliar words.
- be aware of the need for a slight pause at commas and a longer one at periods.
- alter his/her expression for questions and exclamations.

A VALUABLE AND SHARED READING EXPERIENCE

For many children, reading requires much effort, but adult participation can make this both fun and easier. So here are a few tips on how to use this book with your child.

TIP 1 Check out the contents together before your child begins:

- read the text about the book on the back cover.
- flip through the book and stop to chat about the contents page together to heighten your child's interest and expectation.
- make use of unfamiliar or difficult words on the page in a brief discussion.
- chat about the nonfiction reading features used in the book, such as headings, captions, or labels.

TIP 2 Support your child as he/she reads the story pages:

- give the book to your child to read and turn the pages.
- where necessary, encourage your child to break a word into syllables, sound out each one, and then flow the syllables together. Ask him/her to reread the sentence to check the meaning.
- you may need to help read some new vocabulary words that are difficult for your child to sound out.
- when there's a question mark or an exclamation point, encourage your child to vary his/her voice as he/she reads the sentence. Demonstrate how to do this if it is helpful.

TIP 3 Chat at the end of each page:

- ask questions about the text and the meaning of the words used. These help to develop comprehension skills and awareness of the language used.

A FEW ADDITIONAL TIPS

- Always encourage your child to try reading difficult words by themselves. Praise any self-corrections, for example, "I like the way you sounded out that word and then changed the way you said it, to make sense."
- Try to read together everyday. Reading little and often is best. These books are divided into manageable chapters for one reading session. However, after 10 minutes, only keep going if your child wants to read on.
- Read other books of different types to your child just for enjoyment and information.

Series consultant, **Dr. Linda Gambrell**, Distinguished Professor of Education at Clemson University, has served as President of the National Reading Conference, the College Reading Association, and the International Reading Association.

Index

Answers to the Pirate Quiz:
1. Ahoy, matey!; 2. Edward Teach; 3. Put up the sails; 4. Hammock; 5. Pirates' flag.